EVERYDAY FLOWERS

EVERYDAY FLOWERS

KALPANA ASOK

International Psychoanalytic Books (IPBooks)
New York • http://www.IPBooks.net

Copyright © 2018 Kalpana Asok

International Psychoanalytic Books (IPBooks),
Queens, NY
Online at: www.IPBooks.net

All rights reserved. This book may not be reproduced, transmitted, or stored in whole or in part by any means, including graphic, electronic, or mechanical without the express permission of the publisher except in the case of brief quotations embodied in critical articles and reviews.

Book design by Euan Monaghan

ISBN: 978-1-7320533-5-9

To

My Kishore

Who uplifts my Dreaming

With thanks to Dr. Thomas Ogden and the weekly writing group for support, encouragement, and gentle feedback, where I have extended and deepened my appreciation of both poetry and prose.

CONTENTS

1. LINDEN WALK 1
2. SCRITCH SKRATCH SWEEP SWEEP 3
3. AUNTY JI 4
4. AMERICANS 6
5. MONDAY MORNING PEACE 8
6. BUZZED 9
7. REASON SLEEPS 10
8. FEELS LIKE RAIN 12
9. ALIVE 13
10. FIRE IN THE HEART 14
11. WARMTH 15
12. HOPE DIED 18
13. MORTALITY 19
14. BACKWATER BREEZES 20
15. TWO CHAIRS 21
16. THE HEART IS A LONELY HUNTER 22
17. WHAT TO WEAR IN A FOREIGN LANGUAGE ... 23
18. RAW 24
19. SALE-PENDING SIGN 25
20. MIGRAINE SPIRITS 26
21. GIRLFRIENDS 27
22. TIGER PRESERVE 28
23. BACK OF BEYOND 29
24. TRAUMA JAR 31
25. *I CAN'T BREATHE, I CAN'T BREATHE* 32
26. THE EYES HAVE IT 33
27. WORD CATCHING 34
28. STEAMING 35
29. POSTAGE STAMPS 37
30. TENDERLY 39

LINDEN WALK

Hello
My name is
Bharat Desai

Hello
My name is
Pramod Jain

Hello
My name is
Arun Hebbur

Hello
My name is
Kishore Seshadri

Blue-edged
White labels
A foreign way
To say hello

The stickers
lined up
stare back
from dresser mirror

impossible to see
behind them
even a street
called a Walk

Hello,
My name is
Culp uh nah
I am here,
To stay
No one else claimed
&
Swept the sidewalk

Dear Ethel, Thank you for the lemonade and the visits on your porch.

SCRITCH SKRATCH SWEEP SWEEP

Chinese-Indian broom
Is whisper soft
Grass fibres yield tender
Shedding dust when new
Cleaning kitchen floors
For bare feet and souls

Big American brooms
Straight long motions
So foreign but true
Two hands needed
Capably facing forward
The world outside awaits

Different bodies
New life dances
Inside and Outside
Soul and Body
From Old country
To freshnew home

AUNTY JI

A weekend walk
 in the Big city
Jaunty
spring in my steps
Happy
in the sunshine
golden
A day of freedom
 just exploring

"Aunty Ji!"
 Outbursts stranger
Quick-flash
 of happiness
races across his face
Embarrassment
 lasts a second
Wistfulness lingers
 in the wave after

I slow smile
 at his now radiant
"Namaste Ji!"
Take in
the pale
 worried woman
 at his side

My Namaste
my familiar
features
have jolted
out Real
Homesick
Heartsick loss
finding today
unbidden
Happiness

AMERICANS

Chatty American
different baseball cap
every day
it is *Tanzania* today
full of information
what's on the phone
news
open
friendly

It is cold out today
It is cold out today
Sometimes they hear
Sometimes, they don't

Happy New Year
he tries, in September
Persian friend nods
handing pieces out
from his bag
full of cut fruit
at intervals
to his friends

Malaysian man
with Chinese newspaper
reading quietly
speaking rarely
Indian man
tall and albino
not here today
his chair empty

After snacks and coffee
they talk more
Persian and American

Four friends
at their everyday table
at their everyday café
They can still get to the café
The gang of four

MONDAY MORNING PEACE

Key turns
door squeaks
walking in
weightless calm

watering plants
fluffing cushions
clicking lamps
folding papers

Sinking in
chair is cool
couches frame
warm rugs
clear table

silent
spaces
echo
my own.

BUZZED

Purring thrumming
engine in the sky
I am buzzed
lying
in a hammock
Blue and white
dragonfly
tilts a wing
Is it you
I wonder
showing love

REASON SLEEPS

Mother
is lost
Once again
looks down
Why
this shabby
Where
my gorgeous silks
Sarees
proudly collected

Time
to be quiet
Something
here is
A savage
waking garden
A spell to undo
Morning
be here soon
Morning
be here soon

Tea time
brings
a cheerful stranger
Bring me
a mirror
Patients
be here soon

Who is this?
Why
are y*ou* here
When
did you get here

My mother's
in my mirror
is she walled in
am i locked out
And
where are *my* silks
Morning be here soon
Please.

FEELS LIKE RAIN

Pungent-sweet
flaming
scarlet avenue
Green
gul Mohur buds
pop underfoot
Buzzing cicadas
humm hypnotic
backnotes to
too-loud birdsong
Bougainvillea has
remembered thorns
Dry purple blooms
peel off the floor
Gravel sizzles
hopping feet

Philosophic vigil
On bathroom floor
Dog's tongue
languor now
Watching waiting
Waiting watching.

ALIVE

Will I remember
can I recall
this moment
this age
this cool soft air

The enchantments
Creamy Daphne
Pink Jasmine
Yellow White
Honeysuckle

The musical stream
Gravel underfoot
It is a blessing time

I will myself
I will
hold it tight
in a sieve
and
Remember.

FIRE IN THE HEART

There's a fire in the heart
laughter makes hotter
Light in the eyes
pushes them younger
Evening and morning
their piece of moonlight

Whiffs of sea-spray
salty on the lips
Whale breeches
There there
where where
look look
oohs aahs
Again, again
let's do it again
Never-growing-up
with
their child-forever

Moonshadow eats
Sun into diamond
Creating a hush
Breathless and awed
oohs aahs
Again, again
let's do it again
Never-growing-up
with their child-forever

No one
not anyone
Can touch hear smell
The fires in hearts
locked worlds
journeys
pilgrimages
In grace.

WARMTH

A flannel shirt
still hot from the dryer

Immersive heat
in a baked car
on a windy day

A steaming bath

A coarse sun-dried towel

Snapping fire
cinders flying

Nothing matches
no equal to
A flung-body hug

Arms locked
around neck

Faces mashed
Grinding teeth

I love you
I love you
Face Squeezed
Fish lips

Piercing eyes
Noses smushed
Locking eyes

Amma,
Are you listening?
Amma?

I love you.

HOPE DIED

One brown leather bag
Zipped tight-packed
Other of brown paper
Ready for journey

Baby welcome gifts
Some still wrapped
Others washed naked
Hastily folded goodbyes

Bushy in the bassinet
Eyes turned in
Soft silky hair aplenty
Find nurses' sympathy

Will she be toddler
In a teenage body
Will the foster
Love her tender

MORTALITY.

Fat little cloud
Floated
In

to garden

Bamboos
catch it
gleefully
swaying

Too late
for camera
immortality —
long
wisps
blow by

BACKWATER BREEZES

Gentle
gentle breezes
carry Caawing
Diving Crows
Flappingly predict
Fish flip-flopping
In Chinese fishing nets –
What to steal
Before he walks the plank?

Shrill birdcalls
pierce-edit
harsh crow-speak
Insect hums are
third accompanists
Backwaters slap-slap
the canal walls
Rhythmic backdrop
to afternoon torpor

Rare peace and quiet
 in the noisy city
Water sounds lull
Walled spaces insulate
While the household rests
in the post-lunch drowse
The cook rises
To
cater the rest of the day.

TWO CHAIRS

White-washed
beach house
Red geraniums
splash
Brick-laid
careful paths
To longed-for
Restyears

Pottering
garden couple
Decades long
bridge partners
Different quiets
Sunrise terrace
Unites
chatty & quiet

No more
hammering projects
New-house
settling done
Wood dust
Fresh paint
Still linger
Rip-off-quick
goodbye-cancer
Two sad
white chairs
huddle in
mourning terrace.

THE HEART IS A LONELY HUNTER

Yellow trembling
patches
light
Soft silver
ringing bells
Sounds
A slow-rocking
chair

Now full
of books
& worrying
Left behind
days of
don't-love
no-peace

Left behind
Resentment
Most precious
flower of poverty
like finding
An Octopus
&
putting socks on it

With thanks to Carson McCullers' *The Heart is a Lonely Hunter*, where all the above phrases occur in different contexts.

WHAT TO WEAR IN A FOREIGN LANGUAGE

Skimpy
Foreign
innocent
Freedom
movement
youth rules
Unbalanced
older man
stalks
the bunny

Orthodox
bearded tiger
"Na Khoh Izzhar"
Interposes
his body
barreling elder
off of Tramvai
&
closes eyes
slowly
at frozen
mother rabbit

RAW

The look that lingers
Fractions too long
The look
that passes
Over and through
The too-quickly
Averted eyes

How do you speak
So Well
so exotic
so spiritual
so calm
Where Learn it
Were you,
born with it?

Do you know
Slough and Slough?
You do ?
Ahhh... okay
Now I can use it
In my verse
And worse
For everyone

SALE-PENDING SIGN

The olds are moving
Moving back to Japan
After *all* these years
These plenty long years

They have no children
Never open front door
bare empty   yard
windows are shut tight

She went - to work (?)
In & out through garage
sad nods hello when
eyes meet eyes

One time only
He opened the door
Unlocking slowly
Seven creaky bolts
To take his letter
Misdelivered to me

Did
He never leave the war
Did
The war never leave him
Will
He find peace in Japan
Will
They find a piece of him there?

MIGRAINE SPIRITS

In the killing fields of the Khmer
slaughters sometimes incomplete
Thinking too toomuch
thoughts with Cambodian forbears
Emerging clouds of fireflies
scintillate into ghosts

Passive prisoners of trauma
locked in sleep
though awake
Buddhist amulets protect
but
falling prevails

Hungry Khamaoch linger
Approach and chase
Malodorous Chills
Horripilations
warnings of Summons -
Soul dislodgment

White people medicines
Chase Aap spirits
Loving kindness flows
From hearts More powerful
Like water to the uneasy dead
Favorite foods are offered
and Buddha protects the bed

GIRLFRIENDS

Early morning drop-offs
coffee and tea
Laughter, sighs,
teacher-gift stories
Can-you-believe-it
that's what he said
Books, new smiles
how-are-you talk

Who is going
where-when
dates impossible
Summer trips
flights faraway
Children's plans
knit friemilies close

Shining new graduates
Sweet bursting pride
Where-are-you-going
how-do-you like-it
New friends to gather
Oh places to go
These patched evenings
end tender support.

TIGER PRESERVE

Lurching blind-drunk female
in the middle of the day
Slapping holy ground facing
stolid
stony
grama-devatas
Cursing man stares down
Stone gods
fumbling for rocks
to throw at them
in vain

Primal lumps of god
Shrouded
in vermilion Kumkuma
garlanded
with blue Floss
flowers closed in the rain
Are unmoving
& unmoved

Villagers whisper
an only-child
dead
grisly
animal-accident
leave the couple
sadly alone

Dust-settling
cloud bursts
&
Seal Tempers
muggy heat.

BACK OF BEYOND

Snake river canyons
Boatmen have bravado
these
Rapids river guides
have
Ice in their blood
Steel in their nerves

Fast waters
Un hurried people
live on the water
their red necks
sunburnt leathery
with
long long stories
and
plenty plenty time

Tough sharp-eyed
flinty men
raid the river
read it well
Sinewy strength
coats fearsome
White waters

Fireside cookouts
swapping stories
some tall some not
Then a rock change
in the current
slows time

Woman wearing
shalwar kameez in
town's local market
Looks nudges
harsh words thrown
nine eleven terrorist
Looking down
shame & anger
boiling water
drifting helpless
drafting eyes
look away

Boatman speaks
I will stand with you
in market and street
will point out
volatile wildflowers
share river-time
brown hand and white
worn words on shirt
Safe with me
River resistance
lives
in his misty eyes.

TRAUMA JAR

Shrieking grief
Death of a baby
Two mothers
one baby
Shared grief
partial joy

Caring sisters
open child
Pour in loss
Pour in love
Weave in to
Patchwork doll

Now
Warrior woman
Charges shadows
perma-inked
in her heart
Fighting demons
slashing villains
shape shifters
hurting hearts

Care of infants
Holding
Watching
hurt babies
Salve and balm
in her trauma jar.

I CAN'T BREATHE
I CAN'T BREATHE

I can't breathe
  I raise a fist
I can't breathe
  I take a knee
I can't breathe
  BlackLivesMatter is reall
I can't breathe
  Rainbows are true
I can't breathe
  Money for power
I can't breathe
  Yes, metoo

What does it take?
When will you believe?
Here be heroes.
Quiet like

THE EYES HAVE IT

Give me
Your eyes
Full
Greetings
all kinds

Warmth
welcome
Shyness
waiting
Twinkling
laughter
Grace mosttimes
Kindness always

A dozen muscles
A hundred feelings

World
inTo
World
It matters
To me

WORD CATCHING

Finding myself
On a Friday morning
In a crazy-quilt
Clattering café
Languages aplenty
Right here
In the valley

Ar-rre vhy yaar
Let's share it no
Two by three is fine
Nono take take
Come here only
What for to rush

Too many years
Away is herenow
What was usual
Is outthere now
Anew via ears
&
Back into hearts.

STEAMING

Wispy threads
steam
Water soothes
Drifts
tobacco rise,
Orange blooms
compete
&
lose

Orion's sparkling
but common
Silver belt
Even I can find
when clouds
bow away

Only 2 fists
above the belt
Red Betelgeuse
shimmers shy
Betelgeuse is,
about to die
going
Supernova
yesterday today
or a million years

How could it be
All the miles
our pretty blue planet
spinning around our sun
is only
93 million miles

The red giant pales
our 93 million miles
Imagining
4/3 times pi
times 93 million
times 93 million
times 93 million
One cluster so large
My humble mind
cannot comprehend

Nor
that light from
red giant
642 years stale
reaches my
myopic eyes
tonight

The water is warm-
only a hundred.

POSTAGE STAMPS

Island nations
Germany pre-war
India red to
King George
Times
Gandhiji's
Khadi loom
To
Cricket stars

Three square inches
Havens of order
Clear sleeves
Nestled tight
Old Paper smells
Burst from
leather albums
Shelves upon shelves

Messy world
Heat & Dust
After
clean Racism
from
Cold conquerors

Terrors of father
Never waking
- surgeon's scalpel -
Called at seven
Protect your mother
- fiendish family-

Memories of being
Laid out as dead
Waking to wailing
Brother and sister
Mother already in white

"takes up" medicine
but needs walls
from patients
Children needy
People messy

Philately is neat
Orderly welcome
Refuge always

Treasures to pass on
Rare as trauma
Unwelcome.

TENDERLY

Aa ri ra ro
Aa *ri* ra ro
Umhmm hmmm hmmm hmmm hmmm hmmm hmmm hmmm
Aa ri *raa* ro

La li la *li*
La li la li
La li la li *la* li la li
Laa li *laa* li

Umhmm hmmm hmmm hmmm hmmm hmmm hmmm hm*mm*
Umhmm *hmmm* hmmm.

www.ingramcontent.com/pod-product-compliance
Lightning Source LLC
Chambersburg PA
CBHW071224070526
44584CB00019B/3142